UNITS OF STUDY *for* Teaching Reading

A WORKSHOP CURRICULUM, GRADES K-5

LUCY CALKINS, SERIES EDITOR

GRADE 5

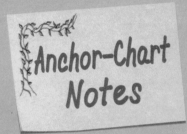

Anchor-Chart Notes

Illustrated by
Marjorie Martinelli,
Jen DeSutter, and
Alexandra Marron

Writing Well About Reading

Ask about power—
...idence,
...wer.

Connect ideas to form bigger theories.

Heinemann

DEDICATED TO TEACHERS™

ISBN 978-0-325-07752-9

90000 >

9 780325 077529

Writing Well About Reading

(Session 3) Read knowing you'll write, seeing more.

Read upcoming text with the ideas you wrote about in mind.

Aim to notice more elements of the story.

Push yourself to grow new ideas.

(Session 4) Use your own thinking, exploring voices.

(Session 7) Ratchet up the level of your writing—REVISE!

Writing Well About Reading

Read knowing you'll write, seeing more.

Read upcoming text with the ideas you wrote about in mind.

Aim to notice more elements of the story.

CHARACTERS

PLOT

REPEATING OBJECTS

SETTING

MOOD

Push yourself to grow new ideas.

Use your own thinking, exploring voice.

Ratchet up the level of your writing–REVISE!

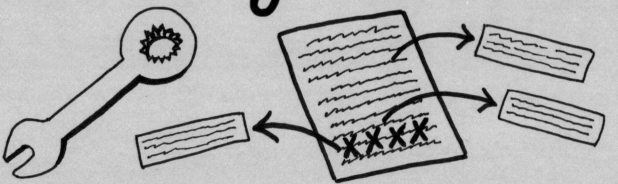

Drawing on All You Know to Read Well & Interpret Texts

(Session 8) Read alertly. See details as meaningful.

(Session 9) Uncover life lessons or messages: Name a big problem or challenge faced by the main character.

Look for a moment when something related to that problem shifts.

(Session 10) Be open to seeing the text differently through other readers' eyes.

(Session 11) Connect ideas to form bigger theories.

(Session 12) Read on, using your interpretation as a lens.

Drawing on All You Know to Read Well & Interpret Texts

Read Well & Interpret Texts

- See more
- Have ideas
- Story Elements
- Life lessons
- Notice change
- Connect ideas
- Different lenses
- Develop theories

Read alertly.

See details as meaningful.

Uncover life lessons or messages:

Name a big problem or challenge faced by the main character.

Look for a moment when something related to that problem shifts.

Be open to seeing the text differently through other readers' eyes.

Wow! I never thought about that before.

Connect ideas to form bigger theories.

idea

+

idea + idea =

Now my theory is...

Read on, using your interpretation as a lens.

Gather

evidence
evidence
evidence evidence

Add to your thinking

Change your thinking

To Deepen Interpretation, Readers Can...

(Session 15) Compare and contrast the way a theme deveops across texts.

Study settings, characters, and key scenes to develop new thinking.

(Session 16) Revise interpretations to make them more nuanced & precise.

(Session 17) Compare how different characters connect to a common theme.

Revise your theme statement to include all perspectives.

(Session 18) Consider the choices authors should have made and the ones they did make.

(Session 19) Study an author's goals and techniques.

To Deepen Interpretation, Readers Can...

Compare and contrast the way a theme develops across texts.

Study settings, characters, and key scenes to develop new thinking.

   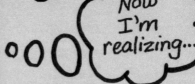

Revise interpretations to make them more nuanced & precise.

Hope is ~~always~~ a good thing ~~to have~~

Hope helps you to go on.

But it can also hold you back.

Compare how different characters connect to a common theme.

Revise your theme statement to include all perspectives.

It's important to remember...

But don't forget...

I also think...

And what about...?

Consider the choices authors could have made and the ones they did make.

Study an author's goals and techniques.

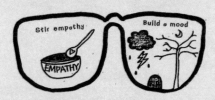

Ways Complex Nonfiction Gets Hard

(Session 3) The headings and subheadings don't help or are misleading

There are several main ideas

The central ideas and main ideas are implicit (hidden)

(Session 5) The vocabulary is hard and technical

(Session 7) There are many complex/hybrid structures

Subtopics may each be broken into multiple parts

Parts can shift in structure

Sentences are longer & may deliver more information

The text is long & connections are separated by lots of text

Ways Complex Nonfiction Gets Hard

The headings and subheadings don't help or are misleading

What!?

There are several main ideas

The central ideas and main ideas are implicit (hidden)

The vocabulary is hard and technical

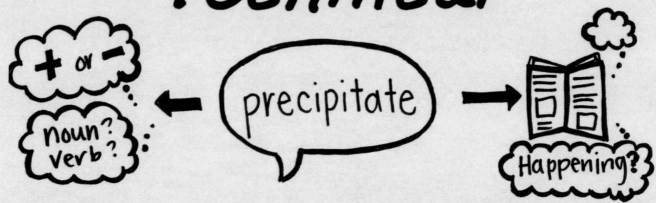

+ or −

noun?
verb?

precipitate

Happening?

There are many complex/hybrid structures

chronological
□ → □ → □

cause & effect
□ ~ □

compare contrast
□ ↔ □
□ | □

Problem /solution
□ → □

Subtopics may each be broken into multiple parts

Parts can shift in structure

Sentences are longer & may deliver more information

The text is long & connections are separated by lots of text

Some Questions Readers Can Ask to Analyze Arguments

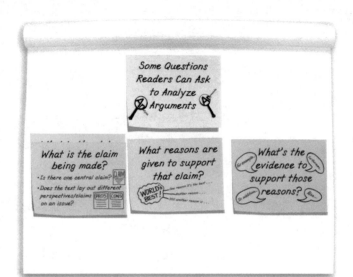

(Session 1) What is the claim being made?

What reasons are given to support that claim?

What's the evidence to support those reasons?

REPLACE What is the claim being made?
What is the claim being made?
- Is there one central claim?
- Does the text lay out different perspectives/claims on an issue?

Some Questions Readers Can Ask to Analyze Arguments

What is the claim being made?

-
-

What reasons are given to support that claim?

WORLD'S BEST!

One reason it's the best . . .

Another reason . . .

Still another reason is . . .

What's the evidence to support those reasons?

For example...

Furthermore...

In addition...

Also...

What is the claim being made?

- Is there <u>one</u> central claim?

- Does the text lay out different perspectives/claims on an issue?

How to Research an Issue Deeply

(Session 2) Set aside your own opinions and suspend judgment

Make a reading plan

Gather evidence for both sides of the issue

(Session 3) Engage in quick flash debates

Raise new questions

(Session 4) Read to understand the issue

(Session 7) Understand what each text is saying & how it fits into the overall argument

(Session 8) **Leave a blank spot on the chart**

Make an informed, well-reasoned argument about the issue

Reflect on what you learned through arguing

(Session 13) **Place in blank spot**
Think, write, and talk about texts on different levels

How to Research an Issue Deeply

Set aside your own opinions and suspend judgment

Make a reading plan –

get an overall view of the argument first

Gather evidence for both sides of the issue

Engage in quick flash debates –
test out and clarify your thinking

Raise new questions

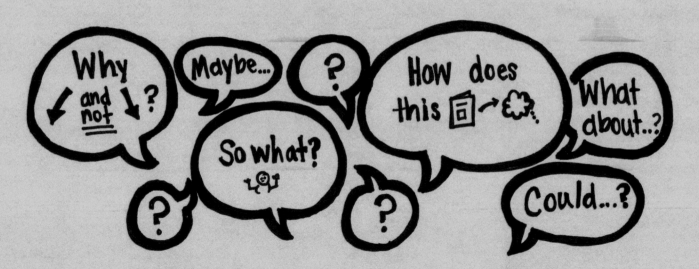

Read to understand the issue –

answer your questions and relate tangential sources to the argument

Understand what each text is saying & how it fits into the overall argument

Make an informed, well-reasoned argument about the issue

On one hand...

Also...

Another.

In conclusion.

Reflect on what you learned through arguing –

raise new questions, insights, and ideas

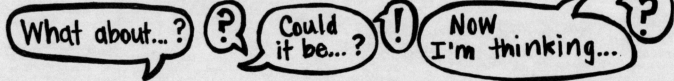

Think, write, and talk about texts on different levels –
consider perspective and craft

The text...

The text...

The author...

The author...

Sophisticated Readers of Fantasy...

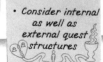

Sophisticated Readers of Fantasy...

Research the setting.

Ask about power—who has it, evidence, kinds of power.

Learn alongside the main character.

Keep track of multiple problems.

Suspend judgment about characters and places.

Read metaphorically:

- Consider the "dragons" characters face
- Apply life lessons learned in fiction to their own lives
- Consider internal as well as external quest structures
- Compare themes in fantasy and history

(Session 1) Research the setting.

Ask about power—who has it, evidence, kinds of power.

(Session 3) Learn alongside the main character.

Keep track of multiple problems.

(Session 4) Suspend judgment about characters and places.

(Session 6) Read metaphorically:

- Consider the "dragons" characters face

(Session 7) • Apply life lessons learned in fiction to their own lives

(Session 8) • Consider internal as well as external quest structures

(Session 9) • Compare themes in fantasy and history

Sophisticated Readers of Fantasy...

Research the setting.

Ask about power—
who has it, evidence, kinds of power.

Learn alongside the main character.

Keep track of
multiple problems.

Character ‚ÄÇ _____

Quest ‚ÄÇ _____

Character ‚ÄÇ _____

Suspend judgment about characters and places.

Read metaphorically:

- ## Consider the "dragons" characters face

Elizabeth — Her love for Ronald

Opal — Loss of her mother

• Apply life lessons learned in fiction to their own lives

- Consider internal as well as external quest structures

• Compare themes in fantasy and history

Fantasy Readers Use Elements from the Real World to Understand Fantasy

(Session 11) Use information from nonfiction texts to better understand fantasy stories.

(Session 12) Use vocabulary strategies to figure out unfamiliar words.

(Session 14) Understand that, similar to real people, fantasy characters are complex.

Find possible symbols (images, objects, characters, settings)

(Session 15) Interpret metaphors and allegories in fantasy stories. Use those insights to better understand the real world.

Fantasy Readers Use Elements from the Real World to Understand Fantasy
(and sometimes vice versa)

Use information from nonfiction texts to better understand fantasy stories.

Use vocabulary strategies to figure out unfamiliar words.

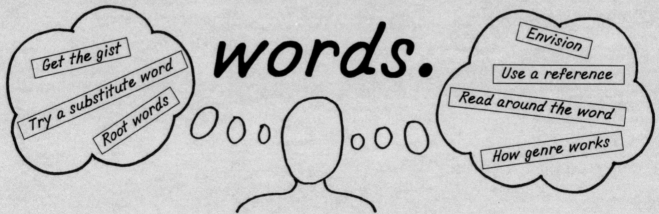

Get the gist

Try a substitute word

Root words

Envision

Use a reference

Read around the word

How genre works

Understand that, similar to real people, fantasy characters are complex.

Find possible symbols
(images, objects, characters, settings)

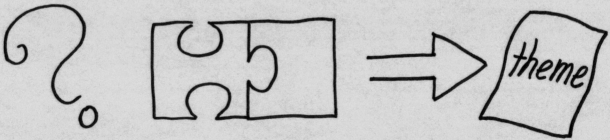

Interpret metaphors and allegories in fantasy stories.

Use those insights to better understand the real world.

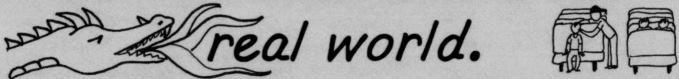

Expert Fantasy Readers Dig Deeper to Unearth the Hidden Layers of ALL Texts

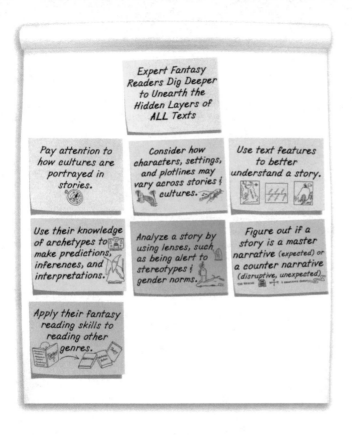

(Session 16) Pay attention to how cultures are portrayed in stories.

Consider how characters, settings, and plotlines may vary across stories & cultures.

Use text features to better understand a story.

(Session 17) Use their knowledge of archetypes to make predictions, inferences, and interpretations.

(Session 18) Analyze a story by using lenses, such as being alert to stereotypes & gender norms.

Figure out if a story is a master narrative (expected) or a counter narrative (disruptive, unexpected)

(Session 19) Apply their fantasy reading skills to reading other genres.

Expert Fantasy Readers Dig Deeper to Unearth the Hidden Layers of ALL Texts

Pay attention to how cultures are portrayed in stories.

Consider how characters, settings, and plotlines may vary across stories & cultures.

Use text features to better understand a story.

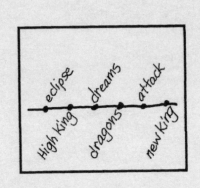

Use their knowledge of archetypes to make predictions, inferences, and interpretations.

STRENGTH

KNOWLEDGE

Analyze a story by using lenses, such as being alert to stereotypes & gender norms.

Figure out if a story is a master narrative (expected) or a counter narrative (disruptive, unexpected)

THE RESCUE 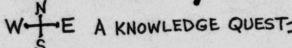 W—N—E—S A KNOWLEDGE QUEST

Apply their fantasy reading skills to reading other genres.

Characters
Problems
Metaphors
Symbols
Vocabulary
Research

Fantasy

NONFICTION

Historical Fiction

Poetry